Praise for *The Power of Questioning*

"*The Power of Questioning* is an important book that I enthusiastically recommend to all teachers. This short and highly readable book tackles one of the most pressing topics related to teaching and learning and is written by a practicing teacher who is simply one of our nation's foremost thinkers on the topic. In this excellent book, Starr Sackstein examines why we need to focus with intention on the questions we ask of students and—more importantly—how we inspire them to become curious learners with a questioning mindset. Starr's book is filled with practical strategies and anecdotes showing how we can transform our practice in this core area of instruction, moving from traditional, rote questions and answers to rigorous, engaging, interactive inquiry." —**Jeffrey Zoul**, assistant superintendent for teaching and learning, Deerfield Public Schools District 109, Deerfield, Illinois

"In *The Power of Questioning*, outstanding teacher and blogger Starr Sackstein shows the way for beginning and veteran teachers to use better questioning techniques to get their students all the way to better self-understanding and productive research. She leverages a great explanation of Bloom's Taxonomy to show how teachers can better use open-ended questions to explore their external world and engage in metacognition. She does this with real examples from other outstanding teachers in a way that should inspire teachers, principals, and parents alike. Although Starr teaches English and journalism, her advice is also aimed a teachers from other content areas." — **Dr. Doug Green**, retired principal; consultant; blogger

Starr Sackstein has pinpointed the single highest leverage move a teacher can make to empower students in their learning, and in this book, provides the practical, classroom tested tools we need to do it." —**Ariel Sacks**, middle school English language arts teacher, author of *Whole Novels For the Whole Class*

"*The Power of Questioning* by Starr Sackstein takes a look at the place of questioning in classrooms today from a fresh point of view on promoting student inquiry. The flow of the book leads readers from background knowledge on Bloom's Taxonomy to the art of questioning as a mechanism for student exploration and discovery of content that is clearly understandable. A noteworthy feature of the book, self-reflective questions, are pivotally positioned allowing for pausing to ponder the significance of the material presented. The insertion of positive teacher anecdotes provides insight into classroom practices that strengthen the art of effective questioning inspires deeper learning and meaning making. The book is thoughtfully presented leading educators to value the practice of questioning as a stepping stone to students' deeper reflection and understanding of knowledge of the world. *The Power of Questioning* is more than another text on the nuances of questioning. It is a compilation of ideas strengthening the purpose for effective teaching that empowers students to become questioners of their own learning. It is a call to action to create avid and passionate learners who take risks while searching for their identity as curious learners on the road to discovery. If we are to create learners that question then we must understand how to scaffold the steps to lead them there. This book allows teachers to question their practice in order to provide next steps for students to grow as learners."—**Carol Varsalona**, ELA consultant; co-moderator of #NYED-Chat

"For far too long, classrooms have been teacher-centric environments, where education is something done to students and not something students help drive. In this book, Sackstein identifies ways to give the classroom back to the students, through creating a culture of innovation, asking the right types of questions, and utilizing technology as a tool to accelerate authentic learning. Quite often the love of learning is schooled right out of students in a traditional environment, yet Sackstein offers ways to combat the traditional approach and help empower students to ultimately take charge of their own learning." —**Thomas C. Murray**, State and District Digital Learning Director, Alliance for Excellent Education, Center for Digital Learning

The Power of Questioning

The Power of Questioning

Opening up the World of Student Inquiry

Starr Sackstein

ROWMAN & LITTLEFIELD
Lanham • Boulder • New York • London

Published by Rowman & Littlefield
A wholly owned subsidiary of The Rowman & Littlefield Publishing Group, Inc.
4501 Forbes Boulevard, Suite 200, Lanham, Maryland 20706
www.rowman.com

Unit A, Whitacre Mews, 26-34 Stannary Street, London SE11 4AB

British Library Cataloguing in Publication Information Available

Library of Congress Cataloging-in-Publication Data

ISBN 978-1-4758-2141-3 (cloth : alk. paper) -- ISBN 978-1-4758-2142-0 (paper : alk. paper) -- ISBN 978-1-4758-2143-7 (electronic)

∞ ™ The paper used in this publication meets the minimum requirements of American National Standard for Information Sciences Permanence of Paper for Printed Library Materials, ANSI/NISO Z39.48-1992.

Printed in the United States of America

For the many questions that fill a child's mind, I'm encouraged to share that wonder with all students and continue to reconnect them with their earlier curiosity. Each day, my son Logan now 10, reminds me of the boundless edge of possibility and why we need to continue to seek out both the answerable and unanswerable. His sense of knowing inspires me, as he continues to probe me to continue to grow.

It is with great gratitude that I watch my son discover the world as it pushes me to make the classroom I create with my students more open to awe. My role as mother has prepared me to support the wonderful variety of learners that grace our shared space each day. Through their wonderful questions I continue to progress as well.

And to the amazing teachers I have had over the years who always allowed me to meander off the path in my own direction. Whether it was my art teacher, who let me cast my body in plaster while others safely drew still-lives or my English teachers who engaged me in conversation about my writing and literature.

In recent years, Joey Goodman, my partner and technology guru has always humored my many questions and has supported me in my journey. He studiously seeks to find me answers and more impressively has taught me where to look to do it on my own.

Contents

Acknowledgments

It's not without help that any person gets to fulfill a dream, and for that I'm grateful. Peter DeWitt has been a great supporter of my work, and it is because of his belief in what I do that I was placed in the position to write as I do. It is because of my connection to him that I first accepted my blog on Education Week Teacher, and through that blog I had the opportunity to write this book.

This book would not have happened without great friends and admired colleagues who contributed to its completion. I'm greatly appreciative to Mark Barnes for agreeing to write the foreword and to share his expertise with my readers.

A big thank you to Jessica Cimini-Samuels, my dear friend and esteemed colleague, who agreed to write a story to share the awesomeness of teaching science and how it naturally leaves room for curiosity.

Thank you to my friend, Janet Schuellein, for sharing her story of learning after I asked with a short deadline. I'm grateful for our fortuitous meeting this year, as she has quickly become one of my favorite people.

A show of gratitude to Connie Hamilton, who generously contributed her expertise about questioning and Bloom's and was eager to help me move forward with the work. She has been available to answer questions and to check in regularly.

My journalism peeps offered great support in sharing their stories about interviewing skills. Thank you to Evelyn Lauer, Kristen DiGorgio, and Lisa Snider, who let the work of their kids speak for itself. Each of you remind me of how we must show kids how to write good questions, and more importantly, listen closely to elicit great answers.

Thank you to Elissa Malispina for sharing her library expertise and willingly offering advice to future teachers on how to facilitate better research learning through library skills.

To Daniel McCabe, who worked hard to tell the right story and succeeded completely. When we put our faith in the right people, there is never any reason to worry.

To Nicholas Provenzano, who accepted my challenge without question and provided me with a great story about how he uses questioning in his classroom in online spaces. I am deeply appreciative for his support in my endeavors and his willingness to share his experience.

To Alejandro Sosa, friend and former colleague was my go-to person for Socratic seminar as the students always raved of the experience in his class. It was a pleasure to talk to him about how and why he uses this technique, and the addition of his story greatly impacted the overall book.

Foreword

The teacher peers across the classroom and sees fifteen hands stretched high in the air. A passerby pauses, curious about this uncanny level of participation; more than half of the twenty-seven teens in this room appear poised to ask the teacher a question. A few seconds drift away before the instructor calls on a towheaded boy, whose enthusiasm signals what is sure to be a take-the-class-by-storm inquiry.

Before the teacher can utter the last syllable of his name, the boy shouts at the top of his lungs, "Seventeen point five! The answer is seventeen and a half." The teacher swings her head side to side, indicating that the student has provided a wrong answer, and the other fourteen children, who were equally eager to answer, quickly withdraw their hands, hoping to escape the ignominy of their peer. "No," the teacher announces. "The correct answer is 16.5. Don't worry, though, you will all get a chance to redeem yourselves; I've got plenty more questions, after we return to our textbook to see if we can't get this right."

The onlooker shrugs awkwardly and strides briskly away, wondering how his time might have been better spent. For a fleeting moment, he was spellbound, assuming that legitimate engagement was occurring, before realizing that this was one more example of a lecture gone awry.

This scenario illustrates an ongoing problem in schools and classrooms around the globe. Some students' hands are raised, and a few are even participating. However, the issue here is not about participation—something many teachers measure by the amount of hands in the air. The real problem is on what this interaction is founded—questions from teachers that elicit thoughtless, rote-memory answers, followed by a great reveal by the questioner: an answer that no one will remember when the class ends.

An array of studies and discussions with educators indicate that teachers pose the majority of inquiries in a typical classroom. Even more alarming is that teachers also deliver the most answers to the questions. Combine this one-way dialogue (questions and answers from teachers), and the result is a somewhat quiet classroom, filled with a single voice. And this one voice, which should be the facilitator of learning, is in reality stifling achievement by leaving our most important stakeholder—the student—left sitting quiet and detached.

Teaching and learning cannot happen without questions. Inquiry is the offspring of curiosity and creativity. Without questions, classrooms are relegated to repositories of empty minds, waiting to be filled with whatever the leader judges appropriate.

Traditional education prescribes a simple formula for teaching: lecture followed by questions from the teacher, designed to gather responses that parrot what the instructor says. Test questions mimic the lecture, and students are deemed successful only if they accurately reproduce the words of their teacher. This was a sufficient model for Laura Ingalls Wilder in the nineteenth century, because progressive education was a heretical idea that people this side of John Dewey didn't understand.

Today, more than 150 years removed from Wilder's one-room schoolhouse, teachers need to ask fewer questions. They also need to answer fewer questions, and the questions they do ask must move beyond "When did Christopher Columbus sail the ocean blue?" to "Why did he sail?" and "Where would the world be today, if he hadn't made the journey?"

In this book, Starr Sackstein demonstrates the power of these kinds of questions and, more important, how to inspire students to ask and, ultimately, answer most of the questions that drive learning. Sackstein's use of Bloom's Taxonomy as a backdrop for questioning techniques sets the tone for teaching the kind of inquiry that helps students demonstrate precisely what they've learned. With this foundation, teachers will find a seamless route to other sections that apply questioning to authentic learning, content-related inquiry, and self-evaluation.

Assessment is at the forefront of the debate about best practices in teaching and learning. While this book does not directly address the assessment process, it hits the bull's-eye that many books about grading miss by wide margins. The best assessment creates an ongoing conversation about learning. This dialogue involves teachers, students, administrators, students' peers, and parents. And when students ask probing questions about content, skills, and real-world situations, they become acutely aware of what they know, what they don't know, and where they need to go next.

Some assessment books are more about instruction than they are about conversation; students take a test, receive a grade, and assessment ends. Other books about grading philosophize about formative assessment, explaining how teachers can use rubrics, checklists, and other tools in order to record observations of what students are doing. Although these are certainly useful strategies, they only begin to address the essentials of understanding when students learn.

Although not writing an assessment book per se, Sackstein demonstrates how teachers can build conversations, using questions—many of which come from students—that lead to iteration, resubmission of activities, and still more conversation.

This is the essence of assessment, and it begins with questions. But how are the questions formed? How can we make our students ask the right ones? Although these questions are asked to ignite thought about this book, they are also examples of the types of questions Sackstein provides herein. She demonstrates many examples of the how, where, when, and why we pose particular inquiries and underscores these examples with real-world anecdotes, provided by teachers in the field who have used the strategies she outlines.

The Power of Questioning is more than a handbook filled with questions that teachers should ask. It's more than a list of studies that prove why inquiry is the best kind of assessment. And it is more than a bunch of narratives about real teachers doing real work. These are the parts of the book— the trees in the forest. There is so much more, though, contained in these pages. So, as you read, don't miss the proverbial forest for the trees. And remember to ask questions along the way.

—Mark Barnes, educator, international speaker, and author of *Assessment 3.0: Throw Out Your Grade Book and Inspire Learning*

Introduction

Each of us starts with a deep hunger for knowing as soon as we're able to consider how things work. Before we can even speak, we question our environment, profoundly pushing objects, observing and seeking answers to make sense of our unknown universe.

Babies knock their cups from their high chair tables and watch as the cup falls to the ground, as if to question without words "What happens if I knock this cup over?"—learning without words about gravity and physics, the cause-and-effect relationship. Toddlers do the same once words come to them, incessantly asking "Why?" and no answer being satisfactory enough. As we get older, the questions change and "Why not?" becomes a focal point, challenging rules and laws as they apply to the questioner, determining what is important in his or her life.

It starts off infinite, grows smaller, and then infinite again as we mature through our experiences, consuming all we see or choose not to see. Even in our objection to reality's shared vision, we assert our own understanding of the world we live in and how we fit into that world.

Developmentally, we are only capable of taking in what our brains can process at any given time, and our own desire to expand beyond what is answerable becomes ever present as our life maps begin to form and we grow into lifelong learners. These specific life moment contexts also provide opportunities for unique perspective and experiences of revisiting information in circular motions. All questions have the ability to spawn more questions, and it is in that cycle that true learning happens.

Throughout the journey of creating this book, I've talked to many educators, demonstrating the power of questions to gather information and to grapple with learning new material and deftly attach it to what was already known. In this way as well, through your journey reading the book, you will encounter many questions that I pose to the reader in hopes of getting you to think about your own practice, and more importantly, modeling how you can use questions in your own spaces to engage students in a learning dialogue.

Questions recreate the infinite in our adult lives. If teachers give this power back to students by directly teaching kids how to generate and explore questions, then curiosity is a natural outgrowth of the inquiry. As teachers, this must be our goal: to bring questioning and curiosity back to formal learning.

With this acceptance of inquiry as a driving force, educators and students must accept that expected answers may not always come, and not knowing isn't an indictment of stupidity, but rather the opposite, offering new opportunities to grow as ignorance develops into understanding.

In all of the classes and contents taught in school, questions can be the connective tissue in an otherwise disconnected experience. Let's put that control in students' hands and allow them to drive the way the learning happens, enjoying the sights as they pass by, toying with the multiple answers as we interact and actively engage in the act of learning. Not all answers will be enough upon first glance; many require a deeper look.

Why not start now and provide students with that adventure?

LEARNING OBJECTIVE

- Show the power of questioning and the inquiry process in learning
- Explore the necessity of a growth mind-set to help create an environment where being wrong is not only acceptable but also an integral part of learning
- Explain levels of questioning through Bloom's Taxonomy
- Demonstrate how to practically implement questioning strategies in classes across content
- Offer real-world examples of how different teachers in different content areas from around the world allow student questioning to drive learning
- Provide opportunities to reflect on current practices and give solutions to improving inquiry in education

Chapter One

Setting the Stage for Inquiry and Self-Exploration

The room is silent. The teacher stands at the front gazing upon the semieager faces of at least half the class. Some try hard to look as if they are present, while others don't even make that effort.

It's time to start the lesson, and the teacher opens with a question: "What symbols did the author use in the chapter we read for homework last night?" And then it happens . . . absolutely nothing. Silence still. The teacher looks around the room wondering if she had made herself clear. "Should I ask again?" Now the students are looking down except for the one student in the front who answers all of the teacher's questions.

Teachers have traditionally led classrooms with well-written lesson plans equipped with canned questions and sometimes even right answers. And with that dynamic comes a very exclusive learning contract between the teacher and the small group of confident learners who will eagerly control a classroom. But this paradigm is not okay.

What about the other kids in the classroom? Shouldn't their learning needs be equally important, too? What if there was a way to engage all of the students in the room by doing something simple . . . giving up control of the questions.

LETTING GO OF THE CONTROL

In a twenty-first-century classroom, no one person should ever be in control. The learning space should be one of inclusive ideas, inviting all parties to bring something valuable to the conversation. Once the culture for learning is established, the teacher's role is more of facilitator rather than "sage on the stage," blending in more readily with the learning that is happening in the classroom.

One easy way to start relinquishing control is to teach students how to ask open-ended questions that inspire further inquiry with their choice and interest at the heart of conversation. Since true learning comes with exploration, and inquiry is a pathway to exploration, we need for students to be the ones taking the necessary risks, asking a series of questions that will propel them forward in their discovery.

Reflection question: Who's in control in your classroom? If you are the primary speaker, what holds you back from allowing students that responsibility?

CREATING A CULTURE OF LEARNING

True, deep learning requires an atmosphere of trust and respect. This doesn't happen overnight. Too often teachers jump into a school year focusing heavily on the content that needs covering, ignoring the most important and ever-changing piece—the students themselves. Rather than dive right into content, educators must get to know their students, develop trusting relationships while establishing a culture that supports risk taking and growth. Once teachers can create this environment, students will more readily ask the questions they truly want to know the answers to.

So how can teachers develop this atmosphere? Start by learning who your students are, not just in school but outside too. Learning activities can be done that foster growth in a content area but also provide personal data about a child. For example, an English teacher might do a reading and writing survey within the first few days of school to find out the reading and writing habits of his/her students. This information can then be used to facilitate book groups or adjust reading lists. It can also help in communicating a shared interest between students and teachers, which often help students to let their guards down.

In the same way, a science or math teacher may consider doing an inventory of prior knowledge that asks kids about how their subjects may apply to areas of a student's life. For example, if students are playing Minecraft or cooking with parents, both have mathematical or scientific implications and would provide necessary data to the teacher about what kinds of skills the students are practicing in their free time. If there is a shared interest in which the teacher loves playing a game or also shares a love of cooking, the student can easily be made to understand how these choice activities can support their skill development in class. They can also start communication and a line of questioning about application that can extend to content learning.

After preliminary efforts have been made between the teacher and student to open the lines of communication, then it's necessary to also foster a safe learning environment among the students. It's not enough for students to feel safe with a teacher; they also feel accepted and respected by classmates.

Adolescents are known for their reticence, particularly as it pertains to self-concept. If they feel that their peers will think their questions are stupid or if they believe they are stupid for having to ask about something that everyone else seems to understand, then no risks will be taken. It's the teacher's job to ensure that the classroom is friendly for all ideas and learning by helping students trust each other.

Trust can be developed in a classroom in a number of different ways. Activities in which students are anonymously asked to share fears in small groups to show that their fears are the same as their peers will help start to break down walls. Students will be more able to start sharing freely.

For more reticent students, consider using Twitter for backchanneling questions that can be answered in class or afterward by the teacher or other classmates. (Twitter is a free microblogging platform that allows the user 140 characters to share ideas and questions socially. Users can access the application online on a computer or from a mobile device through the free app. Students must be at least thirteen years old to open their own account. For younger students, apps such as Today's Meet can be appropriate, or teachers can post on behalf of students.)

Creating a class hashtag can be invaluable in this regard. A hashtag (#) can be made to suit your specific space so students know where to look for information and where to post questions. Hashtags create a specialized feed for users of Twitter and a specific location for students to go to questions and to get answers that filter out other information from a user's feed.

Reflection question: In what ways do you foster a culture of learning in your classes? Specifically consider the activities you do. Take an inventory and see where you have room to continue building a more open and trusting environment with students.

LEARNING IS MORE THAN BEING RIGHT

Another integral challenge to consider in the classroom is the fear of being wrong. Often students won't take risks in answering questions because they want to be right all the time, which adults understand to be impossible. As lead learners start to shift the conversations in their classrooms, a good amount of time should be spent providing students with an inquiry vocabulary as well as a deep understanding of learning objectives and standards.

Having students understand questioning words and providing specific instruction around Bloom's Taxonomy (discussed in chapter 2 in more depth) can be extremely useful when helping students understand the vocabulary of inquiry. Engaging in a dialogue with students that opens up a better understanding of the standards and specific learning objectives offers an opportunity for students to truly question their own learning in a meaningful way. We, as educators, must provide that forum.

There are many ways teachers can start to generate this level of transparency in their classrooms. Consider doing text-based activities that require students to comprehend the standards and then synthesize them into language they understand. Have students post this language around the room and write in their notebooks so that when it comes time to have those deep conversations about their learning, they have a bank of words and ideas to draw on. Teachers can never take for granted that students know. This is why it is essential that they become the driving force in their own learning.

In addition to understanding the language of standards, students must be taught the language of questions. Helping them understand Bloom's Taxonomy and the hierarchy of knowledge will help them begin to understand what deeper questions should look like. For example, explicitly show students that different words elicit different depth, like *explain* versus *tell* or *solve* or *verify* in the questions we ask. The more precisely we teach students to select their words in questions, the better the answers they will arrive at.

In addition to developing questions of their own, a teacher can ask students to first dissect questions being posed into their parts and then later ask them to assemble questions by making cards like a puzzle. Students can then actively build questions that pertain to their learning.

Reflection question: *What kinds of assumptions do you make about learners in your classroom that can potentially impede the learning process?*

EMPOWERING STUDENTS THROUGH LEARNING CONVERSATIONS

Now that the classroom has been established as a safe place and students are ready to learn, capitalize on comfort and press them to take charge of their learning. This initial mind-set shift will not come without growing pains; students are used to being told what to do, what questions to answer and how, and with great detail, and they should complete their learning. They have been indoctrinated in a system that has taught them that their way of doing things isn't the best way. Teachers are responsible for giving that power back, the same way other teachers may have inadvertently taken it away.

A powerful way to start empowering students in this way is to start having learning conversations that start and end with student thoughts. Rather than the traditional teacher/student conference where the teacher again has the upper hand, imparting knowledge and feedback to students, the teacher can now start the conversation before the student even gets to the desk.

Ask students to evaluate their work so far. Consider providing students with a Google Form that asks open-ended questions that encourage students to reflect on their learning and to develop questions for the teacher to better assist them moving forward.

Once the teacher has gathered some data, then the student can have a meaningful conversation in which they are leading the discussion. Here's an example.

THE AUTHOR'S TEACHER STORY

After deciding this year would be the year I would get rid of grading, it was time to start allowing students to take the reins. Realizing early that would create some challenges, as my students had never been put in this position before, I needed to start slowly.

"So, you aren't going to be getting grades in this class. Instead you will be having regular conferences with me to discuss your learning based on your understanding of the standards and various activities we are doing in class."

As you might expect, the students didn't know what to make of my declaration. They looked puzzled, maybe even a little cheated. They wanted grades. How else would they know how they are doing?

"I'm not sure I understand," one brave student suggested.

"That's okay, in time you will. I need you trust me. Can you do that?"

Reluctantly, I think many of them agreed to trust me, and we were on our journey. A big part of our ability to make no grades work was their ability to ask questions, so I had to make sure they knew how to do that. We started off simply.

"Do you have any questions about how this will change the dynamic in class?"

Most were afraid to speak at this point, and I got that. I kind of expected it. I knew the questions would come later, and I also knew the first round of questions would be more geared toward their fear of not working toward an A.

"If I'm not going to get a grade, what am I going to get?"

It's a fair question, and one that can surely open a necessary dialogue, and so began the student conversations about learning.

It was eye-opening listening to what students felt they were learning and even how it connected with the standards. The level of insight they provided me with was astounding. After listening to one or two student conferences, I was able to adjust my lessons accordingly and tailor it to the diverse needs of my classroom.

Students first learn to ask questions specifically about their learning, perhaps in the context of their writing, and then later learn the language of content to ask specific questions of their classmates and teachers to dig deeply into content they want to know more about. It's this kind of inquiry that will undoubtedly prepare students for life as it will engage them on multiple levels.

No longer can we accept a statement like "I don't get it." Instead, we teach students to speak with more clarity and depth. At first, it will take teachers coercing it out of students: "What don't you get, specifically? Can you show me in the text or reference back to something specific we discussed in class today?"

Students will likely find this challenging at first, but teachers must insist on the specificity to be able to get them the information they are truly looking for. Asking the most precise questions for a particular situation is the only way to get the desired information.

Consider the possible student/teacher dialogue from above and then consider one that starts with the following student-initiated dialogue: "While you were speaking about adding cohesion in our papers, I wasn't quite certain of what you meant about foreshadowing transitions. In my paper, I attempted to do a more sophisticated transition as you suggested in my last piece of feedback, but I'm not sure if I'm there yet. Can you help?"

If a student is able to articulate his/her need precisely, a teacher is more capable of providing better instruction and feedback. This is the ultimate goal of education—offering better learning opportunities to every child.

Chapter Two

Understanding Bloom's Taxonomy When Teaching Questioning Skills

There are many questions present in the universe, and with that are varying age-appropriate levels of complexity that correspond to this kind of inquiry. Each teacher practitioner understands the psychological readiness of his/her students and can adjust questioning to suit accordingly.

It isn't enough, however, for a teacher to know the assorted levels and ideas of questioning; the students must comprehend the implications of what is being asked to best suit the desired information. Teachers can model this and then scaffold accordingly, so that students ask meaningful questions that will lead to satisfying answers.

WHAT IS BLOOM'S TAXONOMY?

Bloom's Taxonomy is a hierarchical system of knowing that builds from the most basic kinds of learning around rote memorization at the bottom to creation at the top. When constructing questions, educators should teach students the difference between the kinds of questions and how higher-level questioning offers more depth in exploration.

HOW CAN BLOOM'S TAXONOMY BE USED AS A FRAMEWORK FOR TEACHING QUESTIONING?

Any organizing structure makes learning easier for students, and Bloom's exists in the education world already. Students intuitively understand that some kinds of questions are "easier" than others to answer, and although they may not have the vocabulary or specific knowledge, there is an innate connection with questioning.

At a young age, kids start asking challenging questions that aren't easily answered as the world comes into color. Helping students frame their exploration and put it into context leads to enriching learning experiences on many levels.

In the following section, an interview was conducted with Dr. Connie Hamilton about understanding Bloom's taxonomy in context. The interview format serves to show one way to explore content as well as provide that content for the reader. Interviews are a great way to teach students to question and gather primary information as well as develop excellent communication and listening skills.

1. In what ways does Bloom's Taxonomy shape your questioning instruction?

Dr. Hamilton: It's important for teachers to have an understanding that the taxonomy is not a smorgasbord of questions where the instructor selects from a menu of levels of complexity. In order to reach a level of "higher order" thinking, a student must be able to go through the important sequence of thinking. This journey can be facilitated through the use of carefully sequenced questions posed during instruction.

For example, a question is posed intending to reach the "create" level of Bloom's Taxonomy, such as: "Can you create a pizza box for an optimal-shaped pizza?" In order for the student to exercise the thinking intended at this level, he/she must have some mathematical understanding at lower levels of Bloom.

Level 1 is Remembering. In order to ensure the pizza box is big enough for the pizza to fit into it, the student must be able calculate the area of whatever shape he/she selects as optimal. Recalling the area of a rectangle, circle, or even a hexagon would be necessary in order to "create" his/her pizza box.

Level 2 is Understanding. When selecting the optimal pizza shape for the box, the student must have an understanding of shapes, identify their traits, and be able to compare the benefits of one shape over another.

For example, he/she might enjoy the crust of a pizza and therefore seek to select a pizza shape with the maximum perimeter for the area. Therefore, a basic understanding of area and perimeter is necessary.

Level 3 is Applying. At this stage, the student is ready to take his/her understanding of area, perimeter, shapes, and pizza and apply it in order to identify which shape meets his criteria. Here's where the calculations occur and comparisons can be made that flow into level 4, analyzing.

Level 4 is Analyzing. As the student analyzes his/her options for the optimal pizza shape, he/she uses information he/she is applying and can dissimilate each result of the applications conducted in level 3. Using that information, the student can then provide the pros and cons for multiple pieces of data that can be evaluated in the next level.

Level 5 is Evaluating. Once all of the information is gathered, the student can prioritize the data to evaluate the various pizza shapes. How much dough is needed for a circular pizza vs. rectangular vs. hexagonal? Are there other factors that come into play that have been excluded so far? Here the student not only evaluates information he/she already has but also evaluates if there is any information missing that is necessary to respond to the question.

Level 6 is Create. Now the student is able to aggregate the thinking from the previous levels to give a true experience of Bloom's level 6. How does that impact the amount of crust available for the customer, and how easy is it to build a pizza box of various shapes? Does the shape of the box have to match the shape of the pizza? If not, what shape of box best fits the optimal pizza shape? These questions can only be reflected upon if the student has already gone through the previous stages.

Therefore, it is the facilitation through the stages, not simply jumping to high levels, that cause learning and authentic cognition the way Bloom describes.

Without experiencing these levels to get to "create," a student might simply build a pizza box. The task of building the box itself doesn't indicate it's a Bloom level 6; it's the level of thinking or cognitive application that the student implements that labels his thinking at the highest level.

Reflection question: How can each level of Bloom's Taxonomy generate a deeper level of questioning and therefore deepen student learning? What implications do these have in your classroom?

2. Why should students design their own questions with an understanding of Bloom's Taxonomy?

Dr. Hamilton: I recently heard someone talking about a job titled "Google search expert." We talk frequently about preparing students for the future, for jobs that don't even exist. Who would have predicted that there would be a need for a person to become an expert at analyzing Google searches?

When we only focus on teaching standards that address regurgitating content and not addressing the art of thinking through asking questions, we will never fulfill our charge of preparing students for college and career if all we do is force students to memorize searchable information.

According to a research report from *Ready to Innovate, Conference Board*, the key skills employers value most do not align with the perception of superintendents. There is a disconnect between the importance of solving

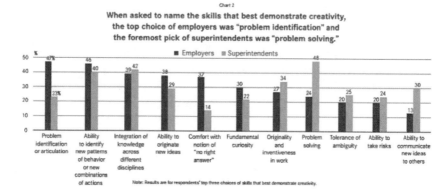

https://www.providenceri.com/efile/3396

Figure 2.1.

problems versus identifying problems. In order for a problem to be iden-
tified, the right questions must be asked.

Nancy Cantor, president of Syracuse University, echoes this idea when
she says, "The best we can do for students is have them ask the right questions."

We might think students learn how to ask questions through osmosis.
While there is a natural tendency for children to ask questions, the older they
get, the fewer they ask. As students approach and enter high school, their
questioning skills decline. Therefore, direct instruction, specifically targeted
at increasing students' ability to build purposeful questions at various levels,
will equip them to meet the demands of future employers.

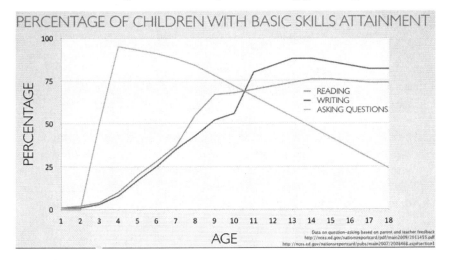

Figure 2.2.

3. How and in what context should students be taught about Bloom's Taxonomy?

Dr. Hamilton: Bloom is the foundation for many teachers' lesson plans. We carefully plan a progression of learning that allows for students to use high-level thinking at various points throughout a unit. Stiggins references how identifying a target makes it so much easier to hit. Wouldn't the same logic apply to the process along the way to reaching that target?

Teaching students the levels of Bloom can help them to identify the level of thinking they are using and why some things appear so much easier for some students than others. For example, if a teacher poses the question: What would happen if we fed the plant a soft drink instead of water? One student's thought process might be at the evaluating phase, which might sound something like this:

> Well, I know plants need water, air and light to survive. I also know there is water in soft drinks, however, there is also carbonation and sugar in the soda. Through the process of photosynthesis, plants make their own sugar for energy.
>
> I wonder if excessive sugar would have an impact on the plant. The water absorbed through the roots allow the cell walls to become swollen, allowing the leaves to stand up straight. Concentrated levels of sugar could cause the cell walls to shrink, making it more difficult for the plant to absorb the water. Without water, a plant will die. Therefore, I predict a plant would die if it were fed a soft drink.

Another student might think:

I remember when I did this in my fifth-grade science experiment. The plant will die. (Level 1: Remembering)

Same question, two very different levels of Bloom's Taxonomy. Perhaps if students understood how the levels of thinking work, they can appreciate how/why different students can be at different levels for the same question.

As Connie Hamilton suggested above, teachers need to understand that by teaching students to create questions using varying levels of the taxonomy, there are a variety of answers, and learning will occur. Students can be inspired to delve deeper in their own inquiry when examining discrete questions that lead to more complex levels of understanding. If we truly want students to reach the level of creation and innovation, they need to both identify problems and then assert the learning in a way to solve them.

Anecdote by Kristen DiGiorgio, High School Journalism Teacher

Ariel is a brand new reporter for Boiler Media and excited about her first interview with Mr. Racket about the school's Best Buddies program sponsoring an event for Autism Awareness Month. She has done some information seeking on Autism Awareness Month, researched some popular campaigns and events, planned out her expert source in addition to several student sources, has her camera, recording device, and note pad all ready to go, and of course, her list of interview questions.

When she returns to the newsroom, her editor asks her how the interview went. Ariel, with a glum look on her face, avoids eye contact with her editor and replies, "Terrible, I barely got a response from Mr. Racket or from the students I interviewed. I don't understand, I was so prepared and so excited, and now I have no quotes for my article and I won't meet my deadline."

What do you think went wrong with Ariel's interview? Her questions did not provoke conversation.

Teaching good questioning is the foundation for authentic and accurate learning; without good questioning techniques, students lack the ability to forward their thinking, or obtain information in a clear manner.

As a journalism educator, I also teach English Language Arts, and questioning is a skill that I teach in both subjects prior to any lesson at the beginning of the year. There will be some notable differences, but the objective will be specified.

In English Language Arts, I teach questioning so that students can have an organic discussion about literature, writing, informational texts, and genuine conversation about aesthetics. In journalism, I teach questioning to obviously help students obtain a good interview for their journalistic piece and to gather information.

Both subjects have one thing in common: they must elicit conversation.

To set the foundation for good questioning technique, I provide my students with consistent criteria and a list of Bloom's Taxonomy Verbs for higher-order thinking (often these also come with question stems).

The following is the criteria I provide my students:

1. Questions must not be yes/no.
2. Questions must use a strong/debatable verb.
3. Questions must provoke a continued conversation.

This criteria can, of course, be adapted to your student's specific learning targets, but I find this criteria is generally consistent for both ELA and journalism. Let's break it down:

1. Questions must not be yes/no.

By asking a yes/no question, we automatically set ourselves up for failure in a discussion. While they may be necessary for clarification, as educators, we must emphasize that clarification questions should occur prior to the discussion or interview. For example: Do you find that attending Autism Awareness Events helps your cause toward advocating for those with autism? Yes. (Now, if you have a person who is truly an expert, it is likely they will continue this conversation, but at the student level, when they are often questioning and interviewing their peers, this most likely will not happen; we must encourage students to cue the interviewee by giving them a verb to help continue that response.)

2. Questions must use a strong/debatable verb.

Providing students with a list of Bloom's Taxonomy verbs for higher-order thinking, we can help guide students to the purpose of their question, knowing their purpose is really the first step to eliciting a good conversation. In ELA, I emphasize that students should be using Bloom's top three categories (analysis, synthesis, evaluation), but for journalism, we tend to use many "knowledge" and "comprehension" questions, as the purpose is to seek and report truth. I often tell students that their question does not always have to be in the form of a question here, because it can be a difficult transfer. Below I will share two examples, one with a statement using that strong/debatable verb explicitly, and one using the verb to imply the form of a question.

For example, use the following questions: "Explain how Autism Awareness Events help advocate for those with autism" or "What are some of the ways Autism Awareness events help you advocate for those with autism?" Here, I am using a verb from the analysis category. By applying the verb *explain* I am clearly telling my interviewee what kind of information I need from him/her. Notice the second example is how I transfer and apply the verb in the form of a question; here I imply that I want an explanation. This takes a bit of practice, but giving students some topics to work on crafting questions in collaborative groups is a helpful exercise.

3. Questions must provoke a continued conversation.

This is the most difficult part for students when preparing their questions, but I tell them that if they have accomplished the criteria for steps 1 and 2, 3 should happen automatically, so it's really there for students to personally reflect.

Once we establish the foundation for questioning, we should then set criteria for students to respond in order to practice it through the use of Socratic seminars or other fishbowl-like activities. You can do this by setting up the criteria however you feel fits your classroom, but it is always helpful to set up an activity to simulate the questioning and discussion process.

Applying higher-level questioning in interview situations provokes deeper, meaningful answers that can provoke further learning for the writer and for the speaker. Our goal as educators is to put these kinds of learning opportunities into our students' hands and nurture the development of their research and people skills by doing so.

Reflection question: How can you implement Bloom's Taxonomy in your classes to explore student questioning?

CHAPTER 2 ADDITIONAL RESOURCES

Bloom's Taxonomy Guide to Writing Questions: http://wwild.coe.uga.edu/pptgames/resources/bloom_questions.pdf
Bloom's Taxonomy:
http://www.bloomstaxonomy.org/Blooms Taxonomy questions.pdf

Chapter Three

Dissecting Questions

Testing has become an unfortunate but integrated part of the learning process, and within that process are the questions established to test students' ability to think. Too often, the questions that appear easiest on the page really are meant to deceive in complicatedly simplistic ways. Questions can lie and easily mislead students.

By asking students to select the "best" answer rather than the "right" answer suggests that there is nuance in the answer. When we don't offer students a chance to explain their thinking and only provide specific, finite choices, we rob students of the opportunity to really show what they know. That being said, they are slaves to the test at this time, and so it is our job as educators to help students break apart the meaning of each question so they can answer in the most effective ways.

When students understand what is being asked, they, too, ask more direct and thoughtful questions. In order to help students arrive at more developed and thought-provoking questions, we need to show them how every word matters and how the placement of each word impacts the overall outcome.

HOW CAN WE BREAK APART QUESTIONS FOR A DEEPER UNDERSTANDING OF WHAT IS BEING ASKED?

On first pass, a student gets a cursory understanding of a question being posed. Too often they read quickly or don't listen actively and then only answer the most salient part. By breaking down the specifics of what a question in asking in pieces, a student can meaningfully use phrasing and diction to seek a better, more complete answer.

Consider the following questions taken from a New York State Common Core Regents Exam:

What is most likely not a purpose of the repetition of the phrase "Give us a peace" throughout the poem?

(1) to provide a unified structure

(2) to emphasize a central idea

(3) to solicit the people's loyalty

(4) to introduce the poet's requests

The poet's purpose in the poem can best be described as

(1) a condemnation of war

(2) an appeal for justice

(3) an argument for colonial values

(4) a criticism of education

Each one of these questions expects a student to know multiple things. They may seem simple on the surface, but really these are deceptively easy questions framed in such a way to get at a prescribed meaning that may be more usefully discussed if done through conversation or even essay.

The multiple-choice question is an unfair construct that both diminishes the value of real student thought and misleads a student to try to ascertain the real meaning of an intended text or problem set.

Both of these above questions were in direct relation to a poem, and the reader is supposed to guess the author's purpose. The first question does a negation that can easily be missed by a reader. The test is really trying to determine just how closely the student read and is able to make meaning of the words being asked.

First, a reader will need to break the question up into sections or phrases to better understand what is being asked. By annotation and rereading, the answers then need to be tackled. Only one is the best answer. Some may be close to right or even right, but not the best.

If students understand how to dissect the question and the answers, they too will be able to see the best answer, but will likely not grow at all from the experience. Questions in this setting often devalue the true power of inquiry and establish a close-ended view of exploring learning through questioning.

This hurdle is a high one for teachers to traverse. It is essential that we take back the questions and help students disassociate these useless forms of questioning with the real essence of how inquiry drives curiosity to grow as a learner.

Ultimately, we need to teach kids to backward solve the questions. First is the need to figure out what is being asked by annotating the question appropriately, looking at the individual parts in reference to the answers being provided and then eliminating those answers that don't coincide with the question at all first.

Although we can try to impart this necessary school skill to students, we all must acknowledge that in the grand scheme of things, these questions are relatively useless.

WHY SHOULD STUDENTS BE ABLE TO DISSECT QUESTIONS TO FURTHER LEARNING?

In order to be successful in graduating from the secondary education experience, all students must endure a growing number of standardized and content-driven tests. Although most would agree that these tests are somewhat meaningless, the passage of them is what makes entry into their adult and career-driven lives possible. So if we can teach kids to adequately dissect these complicated multiple-guess questions, their ability to think in terms of these tests will be increased.

Presumably, the ability to game these questions will hopefully have a positive connection between a student's ability to answer and learn, as well as apply the techniques to their own future questioning for inquiry exploration.

Although a multiple-choice, standardized-test question isn't the best way to inspire learning, there is some value in teaching kids how to read through the words and determine the actual meaning. This skill will be essential to their lives regardless of the path they choose to take.

If we consider these questions an endurance test that is out to seek comprehension more than remembering or even higher levels of Bloom, once a student identifies what is being tested, the quicker and more efficiently he/she will be able to answer the question correctly.

Reflection question: *How can using test questions in class deepen the questioning experience in a less formal, more engaging way?*

HOW CAN THESE SKILLS BE APPLIED TO CLASSES ACROSS CONTENT TO DEEPEN LEARNING?

Although it may seem like multiple-choice questions don't support lifelong learning, the ability to see what's on the page and give the answer that is being expected is something that can be useful. Rather than just teaching kids to answer questions when the guesses are provided, why not have kids think about the questions on a broader level?

Consider this: Ask a student to read a multiple-choice question without the answers. What is his or her initial reaction to the question? After reading and rereading what's on the page, what strategies can he/she use to approach the question in a meaningful way?

First, annotate the question by underlining or highlighting important words or phrases. Then review the context of the question in terms of the others around it and the associated reading piece. After that, answer the question before reviewing the answers. Which one of the answers best fits the choice the reader determined on his/her own?

This skill can then be applied across content and situation. Instead of being the answerer of questions, this can be a useful way to help students develop questions in the future. By giving students the opportunity to generate their own questions, they are more able to see how the relevance of the intended questions applies to the learning that is being tested.

Ultimately, we want to provide students with meaningful learning experiences, and if summative testing is necessary, students must be aware of how to demonstrate and make real connections between the learning and the assessing on the exams. So if we can transfer the skills of understanding questions into developing questions, then students will begin to see the usefulness of questioning in this manner.

But it isn't just students in a learning environment who need to have meaningful learning experiences, so do school leaders both in administration and in the classroom. They need to transfer these same skills to their own personal learning and in a modeling capacity. So how do we generate meaningful professional learning experiences for administrators and teachers? One way is getting involved in organizations and online communities through social media.

Below is an anecdote from New York administrator Daniel McCabe that discusses how questions can be used during Twitter Chats to engage in meaningful conversations that can drive learning within school environments.

Anecdote by Dan McCabe, New York Administrator

In the past, leaders were those who knew the right answers. Today, leaders are those who know the right questions. Influential school leaders ask questions with the intent to be helpful, not to show how smart they are or to demonstrate authority. In a culture of learning, the path to understanding is paved with questions.

For a school leader, dissecting questions possesses a lot of utility, and by leveraging the right questions the utility is passed down from teachers to students, creating a sustained feedback loop. We are all keenly aware that modeling is a best practice that yields dividends to students. So below is a brief example of how I have used an asynchronous questioning method to summon ideas that can be translated into current practice in the classroom by crowdsourcing the questions and using thinking maps to memorialize the feedback.

I have the privilege of being a comoderator of #NYEDchat, which is a biweekly Twitter Chat for educators where we seek to connect, collaborate, share, teach, and be taught. Through the dynamic connections I've made using social media to advance my own learning, I was asked to guest moderate #TMchat courtesy of Connie Hamilton (@conniehamilton). The topic of this particular chat was what educational researcher John Hattie prioritizes as influences and effect sizes related to student achievement—teacher-student relationships.

The goal of this chat was to pose questions that would elicit responses that other educators could use to question their own assumptions and practices and to compile thinking maps based on the information. The new knowledge could then be used as a resource for teachers working with students. So you see, it goes back to no one person possessing all the knowledge. The smartest person in an edchat is all the edchat participants, and by moderating a conversation leveraging technology you can rapidly advance the education profession out of the shadows of its isolationist roots, all while effectively modeling digital literacy for faculty and students alike.

For so long the questions have been locked up behind the brick and mortar of people in the noblest profession—educators. Now through asynchronous learning networks/environments, those questions can be unleashed broadly and massively, tweaked, analyzed, scrutinized, and probably most importantly adapted to fit the individual needs of individual teachers doing yeoman's work back in their classrooms.

Most of the greatest intellectual and innovative feats in history have come from standing on the shoulders of others. Now through social networks you can seamlessly explore instructional and pedagogical topics at scale using the inherent power of questions to guide your practice. Below is an example of the questions that were posed during the one-hour chat focusing on teacher-student relationships. Take note on how dissecting questions like these help to elucidate this matter.

1. There are varying interpretations of the teacher-student relationship; how would you define it?
2. According to Hattie, teacher credibility is vital to learning. What role does students' perception of a teacher's ethos play?
3. Elaborate on why you think the teacher-student relationship has such a high impact on student achievement.
4. Part of relationship building is intentionally focused energy and effort. Describe how you do this.
5. Tell us about a "go-to" strategy or technique you have for building rapport with students.
6. *Respect* is a word that gets bandied about a lot in schools. Talk about respect in the context of teacher-student relationships.

7. Are some students unreachable? How do you handle that?
8. What role does administration play in fostering teacher-student relationships?

Throughout the duration of the hour-long chat, over 1,100 tweets were posted focusing on these questions, and the responses were staggering. Step back and think for a moment about the enormous value in learning practical ideas from teachers who are in the classrooms just like you, facing the same issues day in and day out. You would be hard-pressed to find another way to distill so many voices surrounding a singular topic in education from actual teachers. Not experts, not academics, not authors—actual teachers. What resulted from this hour of asynchronous learning was an avalanche of insights that are classroom ready. I for one was able to synthesize much of the conversation and use it to build on my existing knowledge base and skill set. As a matter of fact, what I have incorporated into my professional flow is that whenever I participate in an edchat I synthesize the information that I glean, and I apply it to a present situation in my workspace.

Sometimes that has led me to share ideas with my principal to enhance our school practice. We should all be idea scouts using the questions and dialogue we glean on our professional networks to improve outcomes for students within our schools. One of the ideas I gleaned from a chat asking the question, "How do we improve Back to School Night?" was to encourage parents to be part of the conversation about the school during their visit on Back to School Night.

My principal, always looking for ways to broaden communications with parents, jumped at the idea. So we made flyers and posted them around the school, urging parents to send a tweet to our Back to School Night hashtag. We displayed a Twitter wall in the commons area where parents went during study halls, and what do you know, all of a sudden the Twitter wall was being populated by tweets from parents espousing how friendly the teachers are and how nice the building looks. The PTA seized on it and took some pictures of the Spirit Wear they were selling for fund-raising. So you see how a basic question about enhancing a common school event led to a great insight that was easily implemented and resulted in getting our parents excited about being part of the conversation.

Sometimes the questions and information learned spark a whole group conversation with the entire faculty, and sometimes I use the information to target specific individuals who I know have specific needs. Several of the ideas that informed my thinking I've used to help a teacher look at a challenge through the lens of another teacher who I connected with through social networks.

Though we are in the infancy stages of the using social networking to level up educational practice, I have witnessed firsthand the transformative power it has. Slowly, educators all around are starting to understand that they don't have to have all the answers. That's impossible. However, being a connected educator allows you to crowdsource—that is, pick the brains of hundreds of thousands of teachers facing similar circumstances. So take a chance, connect with other educators, ask questions, and learn together. It's the reason I've been fortunate to collaborate with Starr.

Being connected is an essential part of teacher and student growth in the twenty-first century. As we continue to make students college and career ready, we mustn't diminish the importance of explicitly teaching students to seek out their questions on social media forums where many other learners may encounter the same challenges and may even already have solutions. Although not every solution will be a perfect fit, they always do provide a starting point that can reduce the process of spinning wheels to know where to start.

As administrators, teachers, and students actively dissect what is being asked as a problem-solving technique, the more readily answers will befall them. If we look at the problem, dissect, generate a series of new questions, and then seek to answer as we go as a community, the collaboration will undoubtedly produce a positive impact on the environment.

Reflection question: *How are you actively connecting with those in your community? Outside of your community? What is one risk you're willing to take to make more connections? Start an action plan now.*

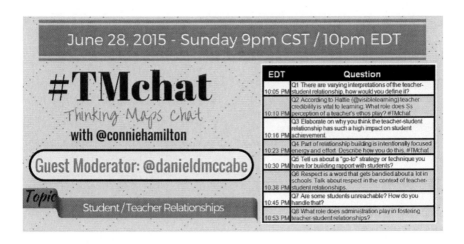

Figure 3.1.

Chapter Four

Building Questions

Constructing thoughtful questions is a skill that can determine a great depth in learning. If we put the power of questioning into the students' hands, then we effectively place them in control of what they explore. Giving students this experience, we can show them how to develop effective questions that will help yield the desired answers to propel future learning in the areas of interest.

Too often, the teacher in a classroom controls all of the questions and therefore maintains the level of engagement based on a predetermined set of outcomes. This deeply reduces the level of engagement in students. We need to open up the universe by giving kids the tools to ask exceptional questions.

CONCEIVING QUESTIONS TO MAP AUTHENTIC LEARNING

How do kids come up with their own questions, one may ask? It starts with helping students identify what it is that really drives them. Within the context of the individual subjects being learned, what do they want to know more about?

If the student comes as a blank slate, it may be a good idea to have choice into their entry into a subject. Entice them with survey pieces that allow them to explore possibilities and then develop questions during this exploration period.

For student journalists, this happens with a drive to delve deeper into a particular topic. Whether the topic was assigned or chosen or connecting to an event that occurred, questioning people and research is essential to developing trust with an audience. This authentic means to learning can be applied to every area and content, especially in today's world where so much information is available for free.

Students no longer only have textbooks or encyclopedias to explore in order to find answers. Search engines make it possible to use keywords or questions to quickly seek out answers to challenging questions, and where the articles can't provide adequate responses, access to the writers or experts is available. Reaching out to these primary sources has never been easier, and when students do reach out, we want to make sure that they are prepared with good questions that will gather great information worth sharing.

OPENED/CLOSED QUESTIONS FOR SURVEYING MATERIAL VS. ACQUIRING DEPTH OF KNOWLEDGE

Help students understand that there are different kinds of questions that provide different levels of answers. Closed-ended questions are those that end in one- or two-word answers and don't provide a lot of space for an interviewee to respond. These questions can be effective, however, when surveying a large body of people and when statistics are being gathered.

For example, "Do you believe we should have a uniform?" This simple question allows the person being polled to answer yes or no and offers the researcher an opportunity to determine percentages of students who answer in either direction.

Adding the question "Why?" to the above question opens up the field for conversation. "Why" questions are open-ended questions. They expect a person to answer with a narrative of some kind and offer stories to share and add depth to a writer's piece. These stories become the quote foundation of any given journalistic piece. The research is then authentic and taken from primary sources rather than secondary ones.

Helping students understand the difference between open and closed questions can help them learn to write better questions for the specific purposes they are looking to fill. Both kinds of questions have their places in learning, but knowing when to use either is essential.

BUILDING QUESTIONS FOR INVESTIGATIVE REPORTING — FISHBOWL ACTIVITY

Interviewing skills are extremely important for a journalist. Aside from being able to research beforehand and gather an adequate amount of knowledge to conduct a good interview, a reporter must ask unbiased questions that don't lead the interviewee in any intended direction. The reporter must be able to listen well while taking notes or recording and then must engage in followup questions where the real meat of an interview happens. They need to know how to think on their feet, and be ready to change the direction of the conversation if that is where the interview goes. This level of flexibility and involvement generates excellent information.

In order to really teach students how to get the most out of their interviewing experiences whether writing for a school media outlet or for a class research paper, it is essential to give students models of what a great interview can look like. There are a few ways to do this.

A teacher can first show recordings of great interviews by famous journalists like Barbara Walters or Diane Sawyer, asking students to notice the many things that happen. Another great example to show that would be of high interest to students would be excerpts from *Almost Famous*, Cameron Crowe's movie about a young journalist following his favorite band. Without prompting students, they should recognize the rapport the reporter shares with the subject. They should note the kinds of questions and the eye contact the reporter uses, as well as his ability to listen and change as needed.

Once classes have explored a few different recorded examples, it's time to put them in a simulation or fishbowl activity. Consider setting up the classroom to allow for either two students or the teacher and a student to demonstrate what a sample interview can look like. Have the rest of the class arranged around the simulation, taking notes. There should be no interruptions during the fishbowl activity.

Inside the fishbowl, the interview should first demonstrate possible areas where things can go wrong and where the interviewer makes classic mistakes. Perhaps the reporter comes unprepared or is disrespectful or inappropriate. Maybe the questions are poorly written and the reporter isn't listening attentively to the answers.

Once the first simulation is complete, pause and ask the watchers what they noticed. What wasn't working, and more importantly, why? Once the students have established what isn't working, then begin the simulation again, correcting the mistakes that occurred the first time. Ask students to watch what is different and be ready to discuss after.

The second simulation should correct the first mistakes and should show the power of really good questions and rapport with a subject. The more engaging a reporter can be the more readily an interview subject will open up to them about their story. The most engaging interviews are those that mimic real, thoughtful conversations—a respect for the answers being given and an interest in the answers.

A reporter should always end an interview after reviewing facts acquired by thanking the subject for his or her time. Always make sure that contact information is available to follow up if more information is needed later.

JOURNALISM IN CONTEXT

In the below anecdotes, see how different journalism teachers teach interviewing skills and develop each reporter's ability to ask powerful and engaging questions to drive content in the stories they write.

Anecdote by Evelyn Lauer, The Art of Asking the Right Questions: A Lesson for Journalism 101

"What's your favorite color?"

It doesn't matter what your answer is—no one cares. At least, that's what
I tell my journalism students when I teach them how to ask questions that
will give them interesting answers. Reporting is all about questioning. Ask
the right question, and your story (the product you are producing in a journalism classroom) enfolds easily. Ask a bad question, get a bad answer, and
what results is boring for your reader.

You can ask, "What's your favorite color?" "What's your favorite movie?" "How many brothers and sisters do you have?" But what does that give
you—except for a list of fast facts. Unless your subject is Brad Pitt, no one
cares. What readers do care about—any reader, every reader—is your subject's story. It's your job, as a reporter, to ask the right questions to have your
subject reveal a piece of his or her story.

That's what I tell my students: everyone has a story. Everyone. He or she
doesn't need to be the quarterback of the football team or the leading thes-
pian or the science fair star to be interesting. Sally Jones in the corner who no
one knows? She's interesting, too. You just have to ask her some questions.
Good ones. In fact, Sally is probably more interesting than you think. Sally's
story is worth being told, too. And you, student reporter (or teacher instruct-
ing students how to interview), get the privilege to ask her these questions.
Because that's what it is—a privilege.

So how do you ask Sally the right questions that will make her open up
about her previously unknown world?

You start small and simple. You observe. You remain focused.

You: Hey, Sally. I notice you're wearing a Metallica T-shirt. Can you tell
me more about that? (Here, you are paying attention to details. Here,
you are asking an open-ended question. You are NOT asking, "Do you
like Metallica?" to which Sally will likely reply, "What do you think?
I'm wearing their shirt." Yes-and-no questions are the worst. Don't
ask them.)

Sally: Umm, yeah, they've always been one of my favorite bands.

You: Why? (Always ask why. Always push for more. There is always
more behind the first answer.)

Sally: Because my dad was super into them when he was in high school.

You: Tell me more about your dad. What other kind of music does he like? (Again: open-ended. You're letting Sally talk, but you're guiding the direction. You're keeping her focused on a topic that's interesting. You're not moving on to "What's your favorite color?")

Sally: He only likes metal. He's in a metal band. I play the drums in it.

You: That's amazing. You play the drums? I had no idea. (You've found your focus . . . now you pounce. You keep guiding the conversation with "tell me more," but you let Sally talk. Remember this is about her, not you.)

At the beginning of my Intro to Journalism course, I go over how to interview and how to ask good questions. Then I pair up my students, and they have to ask each other questions in the same way as I've set up in the above example. Then they have to tell each other's stories to the class as a way of introduction.

One thing I've noticed: students struggle with the concept of staying focused. They get lazy and resort to fast facts because somehow it's easier, or they've been programmed—in earlier grades, in different classes—that this is what it means to question someone; however, questioning needs to go beyond random lists of meaningless information because answers such as "red" and "*Inception*" only scratch the surface. As educators, we want our students to dig deep in all their academic work—and it starts with the right questions. Therefore, training our students to question is extremely salient and worth the time and effort.

Evelyn's story really focuses on teaching kids to gather great information through the questions they ask. Ask a mediocre question, and you will get mediocre answers that won't drive a readable story.

Reflection question: *Consider how Evelyn's example gets students to dig deeper and really get people's stories. How can you engage your students, regardless of the content in these deeper conversations, to develop community in your classroom and your school?*

Another journalism teacher, Lisa Snider, shared her story for teaching journalism students how to gather "important stories" to enrich her school publications. Read about "The Gambling Story" and explore how a student was able to ask the right questions to get an interesting story for readers.

Anecdote by Lisa Snider, a Journalism Teacher's Story

"The Gambling Story"

In what I've come to call "important stories," those that do the service of informing our readers on tough topics and hopefully include at least one professional source to give credibility, former students and I worked out a method of interviewing that I share with my new reporters. It involves the order in which they interview their sources.

My staff once did a story on student gambling. We have a casino north of town, and many seniors who turn eighteen years old while still in school like to try it out because they legally can. One young man was known to stay at the casino until very late, winning more than losing, and it was clear to those who heard about him that he was becoming addicted.

A student talked to a few other students who had visited the casino only once or had visited while underage. She talked to another who bought lottery tickets. This was a small variety of student sources, but the focus was on the young man who truly seemed to most to have a gambling problem.

After a couple of unsuccessful attempts because he didn't follow up at the appointed time or return her calls, my eighteen-year-old reporter finally made successful arrangements to meet up with him at the casino. There, she was able to take in the images and sounds of the place, and she interviewed him as he played. She asked him about why he played, about his highs and lows, wins and losses, what money he used, and how his parents felt about it.

They were OK with it because he used his own money, he said. Eventually in the conversation, he told her about staying there all night, then going home to shower and going straight to school without sleeping. He said he could quit when he wanted. He contradicted himself a bit about how much money he spent, and she took note of that.

She also found a local counselor who worked not only with addictions but also with gambling addictions, and was willing to be interviewed by a high school journalist. Because she interviewed the student first, she was able to use his responses to create informed questions for the counselor, giving the piece a real, "here's what you might think but here's the reality" feel.

That worked out so well, that now, any time we do one of these important stories, I encourage the reporter to round up their sources and include a professional, but to interview the professional last so that he or she can answer the questions that come up through the stories the sources tell.

We've used this informed questioning approach when talking to a doctor about how wrestlers drop weight in healthy and unhealthy ways and again recently to talk to a counselor about suicide prevention after talking to some teens who have struggled with suicide.

It's often also a good idea to go to administrators with such interview information already at hand, as they are less likely to downplay the issue, dismiss the reporter, or try to squelch the story before it has a good start.

Informed questioning is a great way to engage students in deeper learning across content areas. It's easier to gather interest in what students are working on when they select the topics and then research and prepare to talk to experts for passion projects. Students don't have to work for a publication to write a piece appropriate for an audience. Teachers from all content areas can encourage students to explore ideas and create a multimedia presentation to share with more than just their teacher.

Add interest and engagement by making learning public using the informed questioning technique. Where can you add a passion project in your curriculum to allow students to practice these questioning techniques?

For additional support, visit the author's blog:

Figure 4.1.

Chapter Five

Applying Questioning Skills to Content Learning

So how can teachers get students to use questioning in their content areas? It starts by engaging students in discussions about essential questions that form the basis of unit content. Knowing the set content that needs to be learned at the end of a unit and working with kids to develop questions to explore unit concepts can greatly increase student motivation and retention of learning in any subject.

DEEPER LEARNING HAPPENS WHEN STUDENTS ARE QUESTIONING CONTENT

Too often teachers determine the outline of learning in a class. Although most content areas terminate in state exams of some kind, that doesn't mean that kids can't participate in generating questions that drive the focus of the class on any given day. By empowering students to participate in this activity, the level of individual investment goes up and the necessary content is still taught, maybe just not in the intended way.

Using graphic organizers like "Know, Want to Know, Learned" (KWL) charts are a great starting point. Ask kids what they "know" already and map it out using a brain dump in the first column. Then fill in the middle column with specific things they are curious about based on the cursory information provided. Use this column to generate guiding questions to focus daily lessons. Consider grouping kids based on common interests, and wherever possible, allow students to take their own journey with the content.

As they continue to work alone or in small groups to establish answers to their individual questions, students can then fill out their "learned" section.

Generate a list of concepts that need to be covered, and students can cross-reference what they learned with that list. If there are any holes, then students "network with" or interview their classmates to make sure all of the content has been covered.

Rather than use a short-answer test to see how much students have learned, consider either letting students write the test or creating a synthesis project that can work across discipline areas. This coupled with experiences in the classroom will ensure the students will develop learning experiences that are more easily referenced than straight-up lectures or teacher-made questions and tests.

Reflection question: *What kinds of synthesis projects do you currently use to engage students in questioning of content? If none, how can you adjust the current assessment to provide formative opportunities for questioning?*

Another great learning experience that uses questioning is a Socratic seminar, which will be discussed later in the chapter. Students prepare for the seminar and participate in a complex questioning activity to explore more deeply the content being learned. This is especially useful for classes that fall under the humanities umbrella, but it can certainly be used for science and math classes as well.

USING SEARCH ENGINES TO APPLY QUESTIONING FOR CONTENT

In order to support student research on this content area, students can be trained how to apply questioning to their Internet skills. In order to get accurate and useful information from Google, students should be taught how to input specific questions to generate proper answers without having to read through multiple articles or resources that cover the same thing.

Teaching students about key words and Boolean operators will offer students a robust searching experience while trying to gather answers to questions. Students can go on scavenger hunts to find information to start off a unit. Providing lessons not just on how to use Google and then how to select the best resources that a Google search turns up, students can be the masters of their content learning.

Advanced searches also provide more control over nuanced searches that allow students to weed through unwanted information. The specificity offers students a chance to get the best information for what they are seeking answers to. It's time we give up the textbooks in which kids are looking in the index for old information, and allow them to explore a more robust source of data online.

Search engines like Ask.com allow the user to put a specific question in the line that they want answered and it will seek to provide the best answers for a question rather than just using key words. These searches can help students prepare for in-class seminars or class discussions using evidence from what they find.

Every child's question can garner different answers, as it is likely students will have different interests. A teacher may even consider breaking students up into small groups based on interest around a particular historical event, scientific movement, artistic movement, or literary theory.

SOCRATIC SEMINARS AS A CLASSROOM STUDY

Social Studies teacher Alejandro Sosa shared his wisdom of using the Socratic seminar in his classes. First he explains that this kind of seminar builds deeper understanding of learning of content and then shares a classroom anecdote to illustrate how it works.

1. How did the Socratic seminar lead to deeper learning?

Alejandro Sosa: The seminar allowed students to think about what's really important about what they read. It also allowed them to apply the content to answer a larger guiding question. Since students controlled the conversation, they had the opportunity to learn from each other. They de-

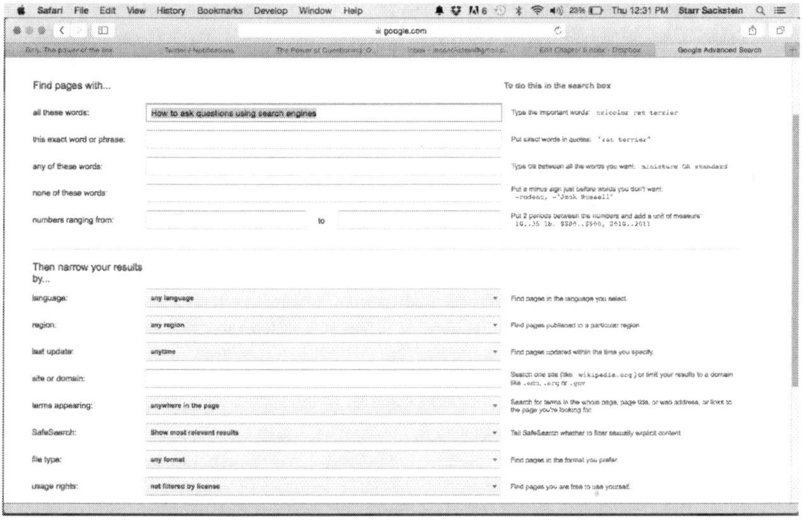

Figure 5.1.

Figure 5.2.

cided the pace of the conversation. They decided when the question had been answered fully. They are also more likely to challenge each other's assertions and ask for clarification about something they don't understand. They continued to go back to the question, asking, "Did we do a good job of answering the question?"

2. Why do you think students enjoyed the activity so much?

Alejandro Sosa: The activity was a chance for students to fully control their learning. It's a bit of a chance to show off how much they know and sound smart—which for some is very important. It's also a chance for them to talk to each other and learn—which teenagers love to do. The feedback they get from me also guides their discussion, and they looked forward to it—trying to improve based on what I said.

3. How is the activity related to questioning?

Alejandro Sosa: The key to the activity is the guiding question, which they were exposed to from the very beginning of the unit. Due to that exposure, students were given the opportunity to think about the question. That question led to more questions during the discussion. Some of the questions were contradictory, while other questions directly challenged each other, leading to a rich discussion.

Anecdote by Alejandro Sosa on using Socratic Seminars

As I think back to all my years of teaching, there was no singular activity more beloved by my students than the Socratic seminar. The strategy is as deceivingly simple as it is powerful. The strategy (as I use it) revolves around an essential question that cannot be easily answered. Students break into two groups and use texts that they've read, any content they've learned, and questions that they create to try to answer that essential question. Below I recall one of my most recent and memorable attempts to implement this strategy.

"That word *civilization*, it doesn't even make any sense. It's so . . . " Miranda looked up, struggling to find the right word. *Subjective* her friend

Eleanor finished with a smile. The students were part of the first group of students having a discussion centered around a guiding question: How do we decide who is and isn't civilized? As students continued to discuss the term and all the different societies we had studied during class, I thought to myself, "They're getting it!"

The discussion continued as students attempted to apply one or more of the definitions of civilization they read about to the discussion. They traded definitions, realizing that all of them made sense but none of them quite fit all of the civilizations that they studied or knew about. A student always ended up saying, "What about [insert civilization]?" and the ironclad definition just didn't work any more. Then one of my students almost jumped out of his seat, and he exclaimed, "This is like when we did the Mongols last year!" (Students at my school take Global History I and then decide whether or not to take the challenge of AP World History or continue with Global History II.) He continued, "Remember how we said they were pretty advanced but textbooks used to call them barbaric because of how they killed people?"

My excitement grew as my students continued making the parallels between what they had learned the previous year and what they were discussing currently. Although I was initially nervous about my second Socratic seminar group, they built upon what the first group had discussed. This group almost seemed to become comfortable with the subjectivity of the term *civilization*.

The discussion was more than I could have hoped for. The students really had the opportunity to explore the content we had been learning in class. They brought in the texts they had been reading to support their arguments, and they seemed to feed off my feedback. The second group referred to the text way more often during their conversation—I can only assume because of how much I praised the first group for bringing in text evidence. The conversation was one of their first attempts at using all of the AP World Habits of Mind at once.

Although the discussion helped close out my unit, it helped create a new understanding for my students—that questions are powerful.

Socratic seminars are one kind of questioning activity that engages students and increases their level of engagement with content, and also helps them make connections to past learning, deepening the level of understanding of the content. By layering the way students discuss the topics, they experience a circular connecting period through questions and discussion that leads to more questions, thereby exploring more.

Although the final outcome isn't known at the start, the guarantee for student understanding of content can be assumed and then explored further in extension assignments or future seminars.

USING GOOGLE CLASSROOM TO ELICIT DISCUSSION

Michigan teacher Nicholas Provanzano shows another great example of how to use questioning and technology in an English classroom. Read his story below to see how questions have transformed classroom discussion.

Anecdote by Nicholas Provanzano, Teacher

Entering my first classroom, I thought asking questions would be the easiest thing to do in the classroom to get students talking. I just had to ask them what I wanted to know, someone would answer, I validate or correct their answer, and then everyone has heard the correct answer and learning has occurred. But, that is not how it really works, and I was not really prepared for how to engage students in a class discussion with solid questioning. It has taken me time, but I have learned some important things when it comes to getting students on board in the class discussion.

Asking questions needs to be about getting students to ask their own questions. A teacher question should not just have a simple answer that comes from a book. It should force students to think about it and wonder about more. I have found a great way to do this recently that has been very successful. I started something in my classroom that I call Silent Class Discussion. By using this new technique, I was able to engage all of the students in my classroom, and they were able to ask the questions that were really on their mind.

I use Google Classroom with my students to share assignments and collect work. I was challenged by my principal to make sure that students are still engaged in learning when I head to a conference. This was a tricky request, but I was able to find a great way to do this. By recording short clips of myself reading a poem and asking one guiding question, students would engage in a class discussion on Google Classroom without ever speaking in class.

The students would respond to my question and then ask another question. The students would then be able to engage in a full conversation until they feel ready to move to the next question. The best part of this format is that more students are able to share what they think about a topic. The students that are normally most outspoken in class were now on equal footing with all students. To my surprise, some of my quietest students were the most "vocal" in the online discussion. They had some of the best questions and answers. It was very powerful to see how they engaged in the class.

The best example happened when I shared a TEDx talk a girl gave about narcissism. The question that I shared with students focused on selfies, and if they are an example of an increasingly narcissistic society. A young man commented that girls are very guilty of this because they just want likes on

Instagram and suggested that those photos should be kept private or shared with friends.

A very quiet young lady in class, who had very strong thoughts on this topic and other silent discussion topics throughout the year, responded wonderfully, "Because I'm not always with my friends?? Because I don't live around all of my friends? Because if I want to take a photo, I'm gunna take a damn photo and be able to look back at it and appreciate my confidence and how I look."

This young lady spoke from her heart and shot back at a point of view that bothered her. Students supported her comment, and even the student she commented to backtracked a bit. This medium allowed a student to share her voice in a way that was more comfortable to her, and it helped build her confidence to speak more openly in class. It was an awesome moment to see unfold digitally and have it pay off in class with more participation.

These class discussions were some of the strongest conversations that were had during the school year, and it was because the students took the lead. What I have learned over the course of thirteen years of teaching is that what I want students to learn is not as meaningful as what students want to learn. Their need to understand will make retention far more likely. Asking questions is not about the teacher telling the students what they are supposed to learn, it is about allowing students to explore the ideas that are important to them, and they can do that by asking the questions that are on their mind.

There are many ways to enhance questioning in the classroom with and without technology. Whether we are conducting a Socratic seminar using prepared questions and ideas in a notebook or Google Classroom, students have the power to drive the discussion in a meaningful and focused way. As students set off on their journeys to grow through questioning, one other powerful tool to consider is blogging. Students can use the space to generate questions that need answering, and the teacher can provide formative feedback as the student begins to make sense of the questions created.

Reflection question: *What technology or pedagogical practices are you currently using to place the power of the questioning in the hands of the students? If this is an area of deficit, where can you make room for one of these activities?*

Chapter Six

Discovering Self Through Questioning

As early as children can string words together, they can begin to question things about themselves and their environments. Using their five senses, they explore the world around them, trying to make sense of the world and their spaces in it. This inherent curiosity doesn't end as children grow into adults, but rather turns inward, and the exploration becomes about who they are and who they will be.

School-aged children have many opportunities to figure things out about themselves during adolescence. School communities and the educators within them have an obligation to provide multiple meaningful opportunities for young people to explore themselves and their interests through activities and school learning. This can be achieved in many ways throughout the years students attend primary and secondary education, whether students participate in clubs or sports or academic experiences.

As an English Language Arts teacher, there are multiple ways to connect with students and allow them to question themselves and their beliefs. Up until a specific point, children believe the values and beliefs passed down through families without question, and then one day, or not, they begin to see things differently as their body of experience expands beyond their homes.

Reading literature offers students the chance to escape into a protagonist's world or psyche and connect with his/her motivations and determine how they feel about what they read. All humanities teachers have this opportunity whether it be literature or history to provide a new landscape to question values and beliefs.

In science and math, students explore the natural and physical world and understand how things work. They learn more about their minds and what challenges or inspires them and start to gravitate toward aptitude and interest, and the specialization begins to occur before it's time to move onto college.

THE QUESTIONS PEOPLE ASK ABOUT THEMSELVES AND THEIR ENVIRONMENTS

The relationships teachers establish with students offer a wealth of information into the minds of the young people we work with. What kinds of questions do they ask us? How do they wish to relate to the older people in their lives, and how do they respond when they don't get their way?

Reflection is a huge part of learning and growing, and the metacognitive experiences we provide our students will help them navigate who they will become. The deeper, reflective moments that ask them to consider their choices and the outcomes of those choices allow them to see themselves in a different light.

What do these metacognitive experiences yield in the way of personal understanding? What kinds of questions are they asking of themselves? Individuals need to understand why, or better yet, accept the place or space they are in and want to gravitate toward. They also help to place the children within their school environment in a meaningful way.

Whether it be through the people they spend their time with or the teachers they want to be around, students are always seeking answers to where they belong, and educators and parents need to be mirrors and sounding boards to help guide them in their search for self.

WHAT DO THE QUESTIONS WE ASK SAY ABOUT WHO WE ARE?

Recently, a colleague reintroduced me to the Myer-Briggs survey and I was reminded of the power of knowing myself on this psychological level. Imagine how powerful it could be if guidance counselors or advisors spent time with students helping them to understand their social-emotional development. What kinds of people are they really?

Below is a story shared by a science teacher in New York about how science encourages questioning and how this questioning offers insight into the child and the world. Although we may not have the answers at the tip of our fingers, teachers need to keep encouraging their students to ask, as Jessica Cimini illustrates.

Anecdote by Jessica Cimini, How Science Encourages Questioning

Why is the sky blue? For every time someone points out this question as an example of an annoying question, someone has asked it out of curiosity and the drive to know (not because of the reflection off the ocean as is commonly believed but due to the scattering of more blue light than red in the atmosphere).

More questions usually follow: Why do the clouds move? What are the clouds made of? Why is the Sun so hot and bright? These are all questions that science can answer (respectively wind, water droplets, and nuclear fusion). But every time science answers a question, the answers only generate more questions that may take years to solve. It is the pursuit of these answers that drives science forward.

Children are naturally curious. The entire world is new to them, and every day brings new discoveries. In the past weeks I have watched my nine-month-old son figure out he can crawl, stand, and pull himself up on just about every object in the house. I can't wait for the day when he can talk and ask questions about everything he sees (although I think one day I may eat those words). And I can't wait to not answer a single one of those questions. Wait? What?

His mommy is a science teacher, and his daddy is a scientist. We have volumes of answers stored in our heads, so why wouldn't we share what we know? Children become learners when we teach them not only how to ask the right questions but also how to find the answers for themselves. I want my son to spend his life questioning and learning, not becoming a repository for the knowledge someone else has discovered.

My son and every other child is going to grow up in a world where the term *Google it* has become what we do when we don't know the answer. This is both fortunate and unfortunate. The positive is, I think, obvious. The amount of information available at our fingertips is staggering. How many times have I wanted to know something and just looked it up in seconds? But this is also the negative.

Too many of the questions that we have are so easily answered that the joy of discovery has been effectively removed. This is where a full and proper science education rooted in questioning becomes so necessary. Science teaches our children to question everything and search for the answers. But answers are not enough. Answers in science must be fully supported with facts and evidence. This always leads to more questions, and the search continues.

Over the years I have watched kids do just about anything to stall a lesson. My favorite method, by far, is the overabundance-of-questions method. In this situation students will ask question after question about the topic (and sometimes about things that aren't even close to being relevant to what we are discussing that day) in the attempt to stall the class long enough so that they don't have to do work. And I have to admit that I am truly a sucker for this method.

I love when they have questions. I love when the answers to the questions lead to more questions. At least two-thirds of the time this tactic is successful in my classroom. The students think that they are getting one over on me, but what they don't realize is that most of the time I have turned the trick back on them. In my almost twelve years in the classroom I have learned how to subtly steer their questions so that they stay on topic and they are being driven to ask deeper and deeper questions.

Often I use the serial question, asking to gauge what they do and do not know about a topic. You can learn a tremendous amount about prior knowledge, misconceptions, and areas of interest of students from the questions they ask. Then you turn the questions back on them and you have a thriving science class that feeds off its own curiosity.

This year I have a student I will call James. James is probably one of the most inquisitive students I have ever had. His knowledge of science is well beyond what most seventh-grade students know, and his desire to know more is exciting and sometimes even a bit overwhelming. When we were learning chemistry I couldn't keep up with all the questions he had. He was asking questions in class that were high school level.

So, after a few days I gave him a high school chemistry book and encouraged him to find the answers. He loved it and would even share what he was learning with the other students. Our next unit was earth science (my favorite and my area of expertise), and the questions continued. This time I was more equipped to deal with the barrage of questions.

Almost every morning I would find James waiting by my classroom door with questions (even though I had his class later in the day). I don't often get to talk black holes and astrophysics with middle school students, and sometimes his questions even stumped me (Google it!). I loved every minute of it. It was a challenge for both of us. I got reminded of the joys of a curious mind and he got to stoke the fires of his curiosity. I can't wait for the questions that come with the physics unit (and I am a little afraid of them too)!

Questions are at the heart of scientific discovery. Since the beginning of humanity we have asked questions about the world in which we live. Science is the pursuit of the answers. As long as there are questions to answer there will be science, and science teachers will be there to teach the generations to come how to ask the questions and find the answers.

HOW CAN WE HARNESS INTEREST TO ENGAGE STUDENTS?

Once we establish an open relationship with students in which their questions are welcomed and explored, teachers can readily begin to adjust learning to suit those specific needs. It is a fact that students are more engaged when their learning feeds what interests them, so as we can accommodate those ideas, the better students will grow.

By providing space in class using tools like genius hour or other passion-based projects (like an investigative feature in newspaper class in which kids are asked to interview experts in an area of their choosing), we can offer students time in school to explore the many things that fascinate them about their worlds. By both giving time and resources to student self-discovery, we offer a real wealth of inspiration to propel future learning. Teachers can foster continued growth by allowing students to step into the role of detective to seek out the answers to their own questions.

Consider the following example of how Janet Schuellein uses a seminar to engage students with text influenced by experiences of her youth as a student.

Anecdote by Janet Schuellein, High School English Teacher

Before I attended junior high school in Queens, New York, learning for me was a straightforward affair. With chalk in hand the teacher presented facts, definitions, formulas, and theories from their well-annotated and dog-eared texts. With pen in hand the students took meticulous notes so they could memorize, recall, and understand what they understood to be knowledge and truth.

Perhaps now you can realize why my most frustrating moment as a student was meeting Socrates for the first time. I knew him then as Mr. Kaseb, my rather exasperating yet beloved Algebra teacher who required students to prepare and to ask questions and to reflect on how they arrived at their answers. It wasn't until I met Socrates again in the form of Mrs. Matzner, a demanding and wearisome English teacher who allowed me to ask any and every question I had (and believe me, there were many, and of course she patiently answered none), that I began to wonder why learning had to be so difficult. It was then I began to embrace the disquiet of not knowing.

Much like my beloved teachers, motivating students to ask questions—questions of the unit of study, questions of each other, questions of me, and questions of their world—is what I am passionate about. I believe students have great potential but are not always heard for a variety of reasons, and that they should be helped to direct their educational journey. Socrates maintained, "I only know that I know nothing." Using Socratic seminars allows teachers to adjust the culture of student learning by allowing students to ask questions and to embrace not knowing in order to ultimately encourage insight and truth.

For example, while reading part 1 of Fahrenheit 451 this year, I presented a seminar question to my students, "What has usurped creativity," and promptly followed up with "Why, and at what cost to humanity?" I used a simple framework to establish our seminar: read, write, and speak. As students read the novel, I introduced texts, including "Peril" by Toni Morrison, *The Great Imagination Heist* by Reynolds Price, *Amusing Ourselves to*

Death by Neil Postman, and *A Culture of Distraction* by Joseph Kraus. Students were then expected to complete the following steps:

1. Read—annotate by responding to the texts as you write, highlight interesting quotations, and write a response.
2. Write—reflect by considering the author's purpose and the focus of our seminar, applying the author's position to the novel and to your world, and forming questions to facilitate discussion.
3. Speak—participate by questioning, discussing, listening, asking for clarification, and taking notes.

After giving the students two weeks to prepare at home, we sat in a large circle facing each other, and I asked students to begin by volunteering a question. In order to enrich responses, students were asked to use textual evidence and to habitually cite authors and page numbers when relevant. Students first began by asking one question and sharing as many answers as they had, which they found frustrating.

They had many questions and ideas to explore, so I asked them to interject as I used the Smartboard to list questions. Visually we began to group questions and to see how "Why are books so dangerous?" easily connected to "What's happened to us that made a future where kids like Clarisse are the abnormal ones?" and "How are burning books and burning people like that woman on page 36 connected?"

Students then began to shape the direction of the conversation more fluidly and were patient when one question lead to a series of others or when one question caused the room to grow quiet and think. Occasionally students needed prompting to connect multiple texts, and I interjected, "How does Morrison's article enhance our understanding of the world Bradbury creates?" or "Where in the text is that idea supported?" This led students to consider Kraus's concerns about technological distraction with Mildred in mind and to ask "How would reading or watching more creative television change Mildred's life?" and "Is Mildred our future?" and "Is this plausible?" which then led students to examine Morrison once more: "What is 'amputated' when writers are silenced?"

Creating a culture of learning in which students are risk takers, thinkers, and leaders takes time. My biggest hurdle was getting students to use their questions, to trust themselves as thinkers, and to trust their peers as listeners.

To encourage students to do this, I collected and used their feedback after each seminar. They requested longer seminars and differing formats so more voices were heard. We extended the seminar over three days and debriefed at the start of each day. We explored using fishbowls, in which students on the inside explored an idea and the students on the outside took notes on the questions and ideas presented.

They requested limitations on participants so more voices found their way into the discussion. We then experimented with a three-card system, allowing participants to speak three times only. This encouraged students to reflect on what they wanted to ask and to reflect on when and how to respond.

As the year continued the seminars evolved. Students began to establish the larger questions to explore the novel and even selected texts from previous readings and on their own. Not all of my students had the same insights about creativity. Some students began see our technological world as a new expression of creativity, while other students feared for the loss of the written word and our artist souls. These ideas later led to more formal reflections, essays, and research papers.

Learning can be achieved by asking questions. My teachers taught me to embrace my ignorance and to ask. My goal is to do the same as I help my students find their voice to ask questions, the patience to explore them, the restraint to listen to others before they speak, and the strength to endure when the answer to a question is a series of further questions.

USING REFLECTION QUESTIONS TO DIG DEEPER INTO OURSELVES AND LEARNING

At the end of every major project, students are asked to review their learning against goals they set at the beginning and the standards the assignment asked them to practice. How well are they doing in that context? What are their impressions of their own growth? How do they know they have achieved or not based on their own growth?

Rather than determine these answers for students, we need to really allow them to be self-reflective and share their own thoughts with us. By offering this learning opportunity before reviewing student work, the lens through which a teacher explores that student's learning becomes clearer and more useful. Imagine the specificity that could be provided to each student based on his or her own goals. Feedback could then be tailored to every child, and each student can get his or her individual needs met while still working on similar work in class.

Imagine if we gave students the tools to ask the appropriate questions of themselves to truly establish a deeper understanding of themselves as learners. What did we ask them to do? What was the process in which they tackled the task? Were they successful? How do they know? What evidence do they have from their learning to support the assessment? What do they still need to work on, and how can they work on it moving forward? How do these needs align with the new goals that need to be set?

Students can practice reflecting and questioning their own growth, and as educators we can offer a sounding board to make sure what they see is what we see. These opportunities for deep self-questioning often lead to a great curiosity about why and how learners develop into what they become. It is in these instances that students may discover what they want to be when they grow up based on aptitude or passion. The right educator, with the ability to just listen and not answer these vital questions for students, can help a student develop a refined and realistic sense of self.

For additional support, visit the author's blog:

Figure 6.1.

Chapter Seven

Encouraging Continued Exploration and Conversation

As we dive more deeply into the areas of interest, research becomes an optimal opportunity for exploration. If we teach students to frame their research around a key question or set of questions, there is a discrete perimeter for students to navigate through and remain focused on so as to not get off topic.

Consider the following example of a series of questions to drive a research paper: What are the consequences of war as demonstrated through the contemporary fiction of the time? How are the historical events depicted throughout the novel, and how does the author apply the "truth" to the writing? What is the social impact of author choice within the text?

Once a student determines a topic that he/she finds interesting, he/she is free to develop a series of questions that will drive the course of research: keywords, what and where to search, and then drive a further course of questioning until the student is satisfied with the answers that are discovered.

Although a potentially frustrating proposition if answers are determined prematurely, the delicate joy of questioning can take the searcher down the rabbit hole of confusion. Teaching students to explore the variety of questions that can begin to unravel as they explore any given topic can be challenging. We need to help them stay focused as they follow their line of investigation by asking our own probing and clarifying questions. In this way, students can decide where they'd like their research to take them.

Teachers and librarians are invaluable sources of knowledge for students. Through areas of expertise, these experts know how to query the seemingly boundless edges of information and find just the right material to generate appropriate answers. And if no answers currently exist, there's a research system in place to start to catalogue new learning.

WHERE DOES THE RESEARCH GENERATE?

Below is an anecdote by librarian Elissa Malespina of New Jersey. She speaks to how library skills are essential for research and in life. When considering the necessary skills a teacher must impart to students, learning how navigate the twenty-first-century library can't be ignored.

Anecdote by Elissa Malespina, Librarian

Why would you do research on a topic if you knew the answer already? Research is all about finding out answers to questions. With the invention of the Internet, research has gotten a lot easier to do, but at the same time it is much more unreliable.

When I was growing up, if I wanted to know more about what I could eat as a diabetic, I would go the library, search the card catalog, find the physical cards (yes, I am that old), go to the shelves, and get a book on the topic. I would then read the book on the topic and get my information. That book was a very reliable source because it had been chosen by a librarian to go into that library. The librarian had read reviews about that book, and selected the book because it was appropriate for their library. The librarians from time to time would also weed out resources that did not have the most up-to-date information. Also, if I had a question about if this book was the correct one to get information from, I could walk right over to the librarian and ask.

Now, things are very different. We can get information in a second thanks to the advent of the Internet and sites like Google. I no longer physically have to go to the library and find a book on diabetes; I can "Google it up" as my young son used to say to me, and find the answer. But here is the problem: Is the information correct or reliable? Is it up to date? Who has written the information? Is the source biased?

We are all about finding the information quickly, but we never really question if the information is correct. It could potentially be dangerous, if I read an article written by the sugar industry talking about how the amount of sugar a person eats does not play a role in diabetes. If I believed that article because it is "on the Internet" and then go and eat all the sugar I want, I could go into a diabetic coma.

Yes, this is an extreme example of research gone wrong, but almost every librarian and educator out there can tell you a story of a student who did some research and came up with totally wrong information, and they believed it because it was on the Internet and everything on the Internet is correct.

The example I love to give on the necessity to ask the correct information when researching is the Save the Pacific Northwest Tree Octopus hoax website, http://zapatopi.net/treeoctopus/faq.html. It looks realistic, with pictures and "facts" and video. People fall for it all the time. When you teach students to ask the proper questions when doing research, they will quickly realize that it is wrong.

It is the role of librarians and educators to help students learn how to ask the correct question so that they can get the best information available.

TEACHING STUDENTS TO QUESTION THE SOURCES THEY FIND

As discussed in an earlier chapter, using search engines can be a powerful tool that students can harness in research and can also pose troubling issues that students decades ago didn't really have to contend with. How do we teach students to question the sources after they have found them? With the Internet being as expansive as it is, we need to show students how to vet sources so they don't end up using something that isn't accurate or useable, as Elissa suggested. As we live in the digital age, these students must be equipped with a strong set of skills to navigate the information they are finding.

Sources like Wikipedia, although usually accurate, can be edited by any-one out there and therefore aren't always reliable. It's important for students to go back to the sources used there to find the true source and then deter-mine how useable the information is. Teaching kids about the exchanges at the end of URLs or web addresses is a good place to start. The most reliable for students are ".edu" sites or ".org" sites. They are usually transparent about who is responsible for the data and are generally reputable.

Students should learn to ask a set of questions of the sources they find rather than just putting a word in the search box and taking the first three results. The first thing students can do is find who runs the site by going to the "about us" page or scrolling to the bottom to see who is responsible for maintaining it and then searching to see if those in charge are reputable.

Beyond that, making sure that there are no broken links on the site would also indicate that it is well maintained and the information is up to date. Too many broken links can indicate old material that may no longer be accurate. It is also good practice to cross-reference information. If multiple sources share similar information, the likelihood of the research being accurate is better.

Consider the following story from my twelfth-grade AP Literature and Composition class.

Developing an excellent end-of-year project is essential to ensure that students have developed the skills intended for learning. Each year at the end of AP Lit and Comp, seniors go through the rigorous process of developing a research paper using the skills learned in class. This comprehensive assignment asks them to take at least two pieces of literature read this year and develop a thesis and a series of questions to explore through a particular critical lens. In addition to research skills, students show their writing process and learn to manage time effectively by taking specific, replicable organizing steps.

It starts with an idea. Students share their ideas with me, and the conversation that ensues helps them develop a working topic that doesn't get refined until after a day of research. One student chose the impact of governments in dystopian fiction. She asked a number of questions, such as "What role does government play in conveying the ideas of the author in this society?" or "How do characters that rebel against the rules of the society get treated once caught?" and "What are the implications of these punishments as a reflection of that society?" Each question is a driving force in searching out answers to prove a point about dystopian fiction through a genre critical lens.

Throughout the process, students revise their questions and continue to search until adequate sources have been found and used to support the thesis developed. After an outline and a draft have been written, students have the opportunity to peer conference, where the peer evaluator can ask clarifying questions to better help the writer fix confusing sections or areas that need more support.

In tandem with the peer conferences, every child has an opportunity to meet with me after they have clearly lined their Google doc with specific areas they feel they need help with. They get a scheduled ten minutes where we sit and review those specific areas. I will not just sit there and read their draft and tell them if it's good. That does them no good. This is the time for them to develop specific questions to be able to get their needs met, and hopefully I can answer their questions with a conversation that will inspire the progress forward.

"I noticed you left a comment about the quality of your evidence, what challenges have you found in getting your support to suit your paper?"

The student is prepared for this conversation, and then launches into a discussion about challenges in finding good sources in the library. "What search words did you use? What were you able to find?" Then we search together in a variety of different places in the library database. There is a ping-pong, back-and-forth effect of the questioning to really help the student arrive at an answer that leads to a series of better questions and then ultimately a satisfying place of sufficient or well-developed support of an idea. Then they go back to work, and I sit with the next student.

Every child needs time to ask questions of the text, of the support, of their peer counterparts who are helping them workshop their research, and then only they can decide if the answers are what they are looking for. Sometimes they will need to abandon an original line of questioning, which can be most frustrating. But once a better line of questioning emerges, then they are back on track.

My seniors in this class are not ready for this challenge at the beginning of the year, but everything they do from day one until their time in the library in May leads up to this moment. Whether it was subtle questioning in classroom-led discussions or developing short papers based on poems or reaction papers written on their blogs, questioning is scaffolded until the level of sophistication is there to do the heavy lifting.

Questioning is the inherent tool of research, and we must spend time teaching students the subtle art of writing and driving inquiry in a meaningful way as they leave their primary and secondary learning experiences and drive forward in their lives. Through research, we are giving students the tools to dig deeper into topics that are interesting to them and explore the great meaning in the world they live in. How can we better provide students with these opportunities every day in class?

BYOD (bring your own device) policies in schools or one-to-one environments where every child has access to technology is one way to help drive this research in the classroom every day. Who says the teacher needs to have the answers anymore? With the use of tools like Google, students can be adept researchers or scavenger hunters of information, and since they drive the inquiry, the level of engagement is much greater.

Reflection question: *Where can we put the power of questioning into our students' hands and take it out of ours? In what way can changing this dynamic create a more engaging and meaningful learning experience?*

CHAPTER 7 ADDITIONAL RESOURCES

Teaching Channel: https://www.teachingchannel.org/videos/teaching-strategies-internet-research

Final Thoughts

If content-area learning are the puzzle pieces in a student's formal education, questions are the glue that hold them all together. In traditional systems, it was always the teacher that held the key to these connections, controlling the questions in the classroom, sometimes with very specific answers already in mind. If we truly want to create a world of innovative young people who are unafraid to take risks and question their environments, it's time we put the power in their hands. The power comes with who determines the questions worth answering.

Although asking questions seems like an innate human ability, since we start out asking so many questions of our environment, students have systematically had that curiosity taken from them as they learn that there are right and wrong answers. Consider the possibilities if we allow them to ask questions, some answerable, some maybe not, but we still let them take the adventure to try to find solutions on their own.

Hopefully as you've read this book, you have taken some tips on how to bring questioning back to students and how to scaffold the questioning process so they can be asking more complicated and intriguing questions in their futures, moving them away from simple, closed questions that terminate in one-word factual answers and into a realm of multiple opportunities and answers. These experiences, like *Choose Your Own Adventure* books, are the true journey of life, tackling the big questions that they can derive important meaning from and then make essential connections that construct a body of knowing that is important for each of them.

Teachers and school institutions can no longer control the box in which students are learning. Instead, we need to create inspiring spaces that challenge them to jump outside that box and grow into inquiry wizards who fearlessly ask the hard questions. As the roles shift, teachers need to show students how to find their own answers, rather than just give them answers.

Technology is a necessary friend and tool to these explorers of new learning. Teachers shouldn't fear it, but rather embrace it and meet students where they are. Textbooks are no longer the answer, as they are way too confined to their predetermined information. Students of the twenty-first century require flexible environments with ever growing capacities like the Internet where literally the world is at their fingertips.

About the Author

Over thirteen years ago, Starr Sackstein started her teaching career in Far Rockaway High School, eager to make a difference. Quickly learning to connect with students and develop rapport, she was able to recognize the most important part of teaching: relationships. Fostering relationships with students and peers to encourage community growth and a deeper understanding of personal contribution through reflection, Sackstein has continued to elevate her students by putting them at the center of the learning.

Starr Sackstein currently works at World Journalism Preparatory School in Flushing, New York, as a high school English and Journalism teacher, where her students run a multimedia news outlet at WJPSnews.com. In 2011, the Dow Jones News Fund honored Sackstein as a Special Recognition Adviser, and 2012 Education Updated recognized her as an outstanding educator. Currently Sackstein has thrown out grades, teaching students that learning isn't about numbers but about the development of skills and the ability to articulate growth.

In 2012, Sackstein tackled National Board Certification in an effort to reflect on her practice and grow as an educational English facilitator. After a year of closely looking at the work with students, she achieved the honor. She is also a certified Master Journalism Educator through the Journalism Education Association (JEA). Sackstein also serves as the New York State Director to JEA to help serve advisers in New York to better grow journalism programs.

She is the author of *Teaching Mythology Exposed*: *Helping Teachers Create Visionary Classroom Perspective*, *Blogging for Educators*, and *Hacking Assessment*. She blogs on Education Week Teacher at "Work in Progress," in addition to her personal blog http://starrsackstein.com/,where she discusses all aspects of being a teacher and education reform.

Sackstein comoderates #sunchat as well as contributes to #NYedChat. She has made the Bammy Awards finals for Secondary High School Educator in 2014 and for Education Commentator/Blogger in 2015. In speaking engagements, Sackstein speaks about blogging, journalism education, throwing out grades, and BYOD, helping people see technology doesn't have to be feared.

Balancing a busy career of writing and teaching with being the mom to ten-year-old Logan is a challenging adventure. Seeing the world through his eyes reminds her why education needs to change for every child.

Contact information:
mssackstein@gmail.com
@MsSackstein on Twitter
Starr Sackstein, MJE Facebook Fan page